BEFORE YOU BEGIN...

Make sure to download the FREE audio program for this book which comes with your purchase! Just go to

www.slangman.com/audio

then look for your book and enter this code:

E2G2QNBY3NZW

GOLDILOCKS and the 3 BEARS

Written by: David Burke
Copy Editor: Julie Bobrick
Illustrated by: "Migs!" Sandoval
Translator: Deese & Petra Wirth
Proofreader: Kai Cofer

Copyright © 2017 by David Burke

Email: info@heywordy.com
Website: www.heywordy.com

Hey Wordy! and all related characters and elements are © and trademarks of Hey Wordy, LLC.

Published by Slangman Publishing. Slangman is a registered trademark of David Burke. All rights reserved. Reproduction or translation of any part of this work beyond that permitted by section 107 or 108 of the 1976 United States Copyright Act without the permission of the copyright owner is unlawful. Requests for permission or further information should be addressed to the Permissions Department, Slangman Publishing. This publication is designed to provide accurate and authoritative information in regard to the subject matter covered. The persons, entities and events in this book are fictitious. Any similarities with actual persons or entities, past and present, are purely coincidental.

ISBN13: 978-1-891888-45-8

Printed in the U.S.A.

Meet the Author
David Burke

Creator and star of the children's TV show, *Hey Wordy!*, David Burke has been single-handedly revolutionizing the foreign language-learning movement worldwide.

In addition to being a performer of boundless energy and enthusiasm, David speaks seven languages. A successful author and entrepreneur, he has built a thriving international publishing company featuring over 100 books he has written for teen/adults & children. His books have won publishing awards and have sold more than one million copies. David's Street Speak™ and Biz Speak™ series of books and audio programs are used around the world by government agencies, leading universities and major corporations.

Since age 4, David has been a classically trained pianist and uses his musical gifts to compose and perform original songs for his TV series, *Hey Wordy!* which introduces children to foreign languages and cultures through music, animation, and magical adventures. He has also composed, orchestrated, and performed all the music in the audio programs for each of these books.

David's engaging and charismatic persona became a fixture on broadcast entertainment channels around the world, such as CNN and the BBC. David and his work have been highlighted in many major publications, including The Los Angeles Times, The Chicago Tribune and The Christian Science Monitor.

"This series teaches everyday words that occur in your child's life, as well as terms having to do with politeness, greetings, family & friendship."

David Burke

German vocabulary taught:

Babybär = baby bear
Bär = bear
Bett = bed
drei = three
eins = one
hart = hard
heiß = hot
kalt = cold
klein = little
Küche = kitchen
Mama = mama
müde = tired
Papa = papa
Schüssel = bowl
Sessel = armchair
Spaziergang = stroll
Tisch = table
Tür = door
weich = soft
zwei = two

- In this fairy tale, you'll notice that some of the German words have a new letter of the alphabet. It's the letter "ß" which looks a lot like our letter "B," but it's not! It's called an "eszett" which is used to represent "ss." For example:

    foot = **Fuss**, but it's always written as **Fuß**.
    big = **gross**, but it's always written as **groß**.

- You'll notice that in German, all nouns (those words that represent a person, place, or thing) begin with an uppercase letter. That's because in German, ALL nouns are written this way! For example:

    girl=**Mädchen** • house=**Haus** • party=**Fest** • prince=**Prinz**

from Cindellera (Level 1)

auf Wiedersehen = goodbye
böse = mean
danke = thank you
Fest = party
Frau = wife
Fuß = foot
gern geschehen = you're welcome
glücklich = happy
groß = big
Haus = house

hübsch = pretty
Kleid = dress
Mädchen = girl
Moment = moment
Mitternacht = midnight
Prinz = prince
Schuh = shoe
stattlich = handsome
traurig = sad
verliebt = in love

1

Bär ←

Papa ←

Mama ←

Once upon a time, there was a [bear] family. The **Bär** family lived in a *Haus* in the forest. There was a [papa] **Bär** who was very *groß*, a [mama] **Bär** who was very *hübsch*, and a

baby bear who was very little. The **Babybär**, who was very **klein**, was also extremely *stattlich* like his **Papa**. The **Papa Bär** was very much *verliebt* with the **Mama Bär**

Babybär
klein

3

and they were indeed proud of their **Bär** family. One day, the **Mama Bär** prepared some soup for lunch, but it was too hot. While it cooled off, the **Bär** family went for a stroll.

Spaziergang

Meanwhile in a town nearby, there lived a **Mädchen**, who was very **klein**, named Goldilocks. She was very **traurig** because she never had anything fun to do.

She thought for a **Moment** and decided to take a **Spaziergang** in the forest. Very soon, she came upon a **Haus** and knocked on the door but no one

Tür

was there. So she opened the **Tür**, put one *Fuß* inside the *Haus*, and said "Hello? Is anyone home?" She was very (tired) after her long **Spaziergang** → **müde**

and since no one answered, she walked inside the **Haus**. She looked around and was very **glücklich** to see a table in the kitchen with food on it!

Tisch
Küche

She quickly approached the **Tisch** in the **Küche** and was super extra *glücklich* because there on the **Tisch** in the **Küche** was a bowl —

Schüssel

eins
zwei
drei

but not just one **Schüssel**. There were one, two, three of them! **Eins, zwei, drei** sitting on the **Tisch** in the **Küche**. She took a taste from the **Schüssel** that belonged to the

Papa Bär and said, "This is too hot!" ⟶ **heiß**
Then she took a taste from the **Schüssel**
that belonged to the **Mama Bär** and said,
"This is too cold!" Then she took a taste from ⟶ **kalt**

the **Schüssel** of the **Babybär** and said, "Ahhh. This one isn't too **heiß**. It isn't too **kalt**. It's just right!" The **Schüssel** was very **klein** and she ate everything in it. "*Danke!*"

she said to the empty **Schüssel**. Well, now she was even more **müde** than ever after eating so much. So, she decided to rest. In the living room, she saw an (armchair)... but not just

Sessel

one **Sessel**. There were **eins**, **zwei**, **drei** of them! **Eins, zwei, drei**! So, she sat down in the **Sessel** of the **Papa Bär** and said, "Oh! This **Sessel** is too [hard]!"

hart

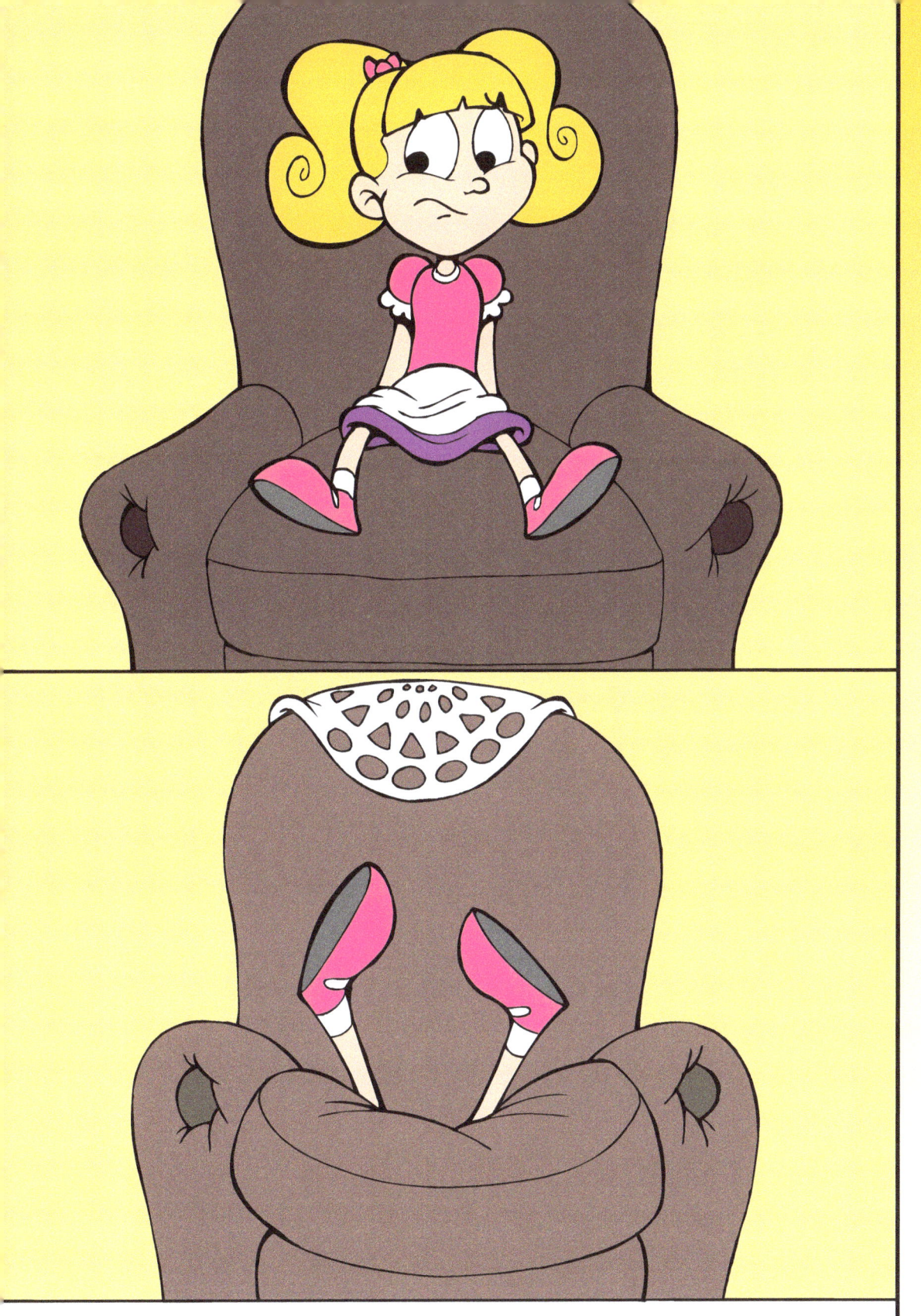

So, she sat in the **Sessel** of the **Mama Bär** and said, "Oh! This **Sessel** is too soft !" Then she sat in the **Sessel** of the **Babybär** and said,

weich

14

15

"Ahhh. This **Sessel** isn't too **hart**. It isn't too **weich**. It's just right!" But just as she got comfortable... *Crack!* The **Sessel** broke and completely fell apart!

Still **müde**, she decided to look for the bedroom to take a nap. In front of her, she saw a bed... but not just one **Bett**. There were **eins**, **zwei**, **drei** of them!

Eins, **zwei**, **drei**! So, she tried the **Bett** of the **Papa Bär**, but it was too **hart**. Then she tried the **Bett** of the **Mama Bär**, but it was too **weich**. Finally, she tried the

Bett of the **Babybär** and said, "Ahhh. This **Bett** isn't too **hart**. It isn't too **weich**. It's just right!" And she fell asleep. At that *Moment*, the **Bär** family returned from their **Spaziergang**. As soon as they walked in, the **Papa Bär** noticed something strange. "Someone's been eating my soup!"

said the **Papa Bär**. "And someone's been eating my soup!" said the **Mama Bär**. "And someone's been eating MY soup and ate it all up!" cried the **Babybär**.

"Look!" said the **Papa Bär**. "Someone's been sitting in my **Sessel**!" "And someone's been sitting in my **Sessel**, as well!" said the **Mama Bär**.

"And someone's been sitting in my **Sessel** and broke it into pieces!" cried the **Babybär**. Suddenly, the **Papa Bär**, the **Mama Bär**, and the

Babybär heard snoring coming from the bedroom, so they went in to look. "Someone's been sleeping in my **Bett**!" said the **Papa Bär**. "And

someone's been sleeping in my **Bett**, as well" said the **Mama Bär**. "And someone's been sleeping in my **Bett** and there she is!" shouted the **Babybär**.

Just then, Goldilocks woke up and was surprised to see the **Bär** family! The **Bär** family thought the **Mädchen** was very *böse* to use their *Haus*

without permission! So, Goldilocks said to the **Papa Bär**, "Oh, *danke* for letting me eat food from your **Schüssel**, sit in your **Sessel**, and lie in your **Bett**!" Goldiocks

said "*Danke!*" again expecting the **Bär** family to say, "*Gern geschehen!*" but they were angry that she caused so much trouble in their *Haus* and the **Bär** family growled

at her. So, she slowly stood up on the **Bett** of the **Babybär**, and nervously said, "Well, *Danke* for having me and… *auf Wiedersehen*!" And with that, Goldilocks jumped off the **Bett**, and dashed out the front **Tür**, running as fast as each **Fuß** could move. Needless to say, she never returned to visit the **Haus** of the **Bär** family again.

Level 3 contains words from Levels 1 & 2, plus all NEW words!

For more HEY WORDY! products, visit...

www.ingramcontent.com/pod-product-compliance
Lightning Source LLC
Chambersburg PA
CBHW042031100526
44587CB00029B/4375